Ascension Notes

Also by Sarah Law:

Bliss Tangle (Stride, 1999)
The Lady Chapel (Stride, 2003)
Perihelion (Shearsman Books, 2006)

SARAH LAW

Ascension Notes

Shearsman Books
Exeter

First published in the United Kingdom in 2009 by
Shearsman Books Ltd
58 Velwell Road
Exeter EX4 4LD

www.shearsman.com

ISBN   978-1-84861-078-1
First Edition

Acknowledgements

Work has appeared in the following publications: *Eyewear, nth position,
Orbis, Stride, In Their Own Words* Exhibition (Sheffield 2009), and
the anthology *Troubles Swapped for Something Fresh:
Manifestos and Unmanifestos* (Salt Publishing).

Contents

Filter	7
Mariska	8
Ascension Robes	10
Memento	20
Gemmology	20
Untitled	21
Box Set	22
Dancing female tomb figure	23
Word Origin	24
Poetry etc. — an unauthorised manifesto	25
Untitled	37
Pear Cut	38
Torque	39
L'inconnue	40
Schroedinger's Mystic	41
A Present	43
In Flux	44
Untitled	45
What It's Like	46
Citrine	47
Meditation	48
An Anchor	49
Dear Reader	51
Sabbatical	52
An Encounter	54
Holy Pictures	58
Underground	61
Mediumship	64
Phase Transitions	67
Lecture Notes	70

Filter

as blue bleeds to violet
    as whiskey warms the blood
        as the clenched fist slackens
        as ah your ribs subside

as a lost glove sinks into the marsh
    and insight drifts into whorls
        your heat gathers and ploughs
            its dreaming, sleep's deep crop

as the night sky's lightpoints
    sink into your skull's thickening
        soup, the primal salt and rock
            (its basal pulse, pulse, pulse)

                            as you exhale

the first glimmers
    as a first bird dares
        your cortisol twists
            tight as a silver rope

pulling you up
    to fields of speech

                        and you open your eyes

Mariska

for an artwork of this name by an unknown artist

You ask for a passport—

                        I say what age are you
you offer me a feather

('just a girl')
Number its fronds, says the woman at your side,

if you would understand
the clock's fibrous delicacy;
        stasis of my ribs, each internally displayed
                a pure caught cry—

Read. You must be taken. *Smile.* Your teeth blue white against
        the sky's
glowering, the slow snap of the shutter.
hushed clatter. Slick ticking of an eye.

You ask for safe harbour among us;
seclusion, stuck poles struck broke from the earth,
the whump of furry rump for scrabble,

(scribbled fury)
                a name dances itself upon you;

        sand or brick-dust lines a mouth like mine.

          Your northern star dilates on leatherette,
            here's the sergeant's stamp:

a disc the size of a bullet's ripple

                                                    (rip hole)
        there is another text, a palimpsest

    stretched across this skin of paper: page's dazzle
            untranslated, luminous
                                        (and crayoned in).

The story's of
Mariska,
an articulate heart,

your power in its flickerbook white cage.

Grace's aura scales your skull: each whispered impulse

            fibrillating,
                                    kissed with light.

Ascension Robes

"Oh, it's too loose to wear as formal garment"
   —threaded colours veining out each zone—
like a rare dance on the skin
  (slipstream riptide)

coursing—

                        as though you are inhabited
by a precious viral ... by a ticking dial
filament of one word to another

—word to another word—

mother of pearl in the breath—

                     ★

"The vaccine isn't difficult to make"

the ache in the blood which passes for hope:
a spur to walk to the next station:

   holy miles, with the foot sole to the gravel and the rosary to hand

—when I get there, I will light *a dozen candles*

— fat wax glowing in a dim lit world—

where beautiful women and works of art are
(latently) sublime

★

a slow motion study of the explosion
(cascade of evergreen dust)

     —your
particles singing a freedom elegy—
for some binding vows
are porous to the tongue—

"In fact I only wear the robes at daily meditation"

             and my hair remains uncut, my name undone

inside, fire flares up
when sitting solitary—

          the pressing wager of belief
          space/time compression
          confession—

★

"I felt I ought to put in an appearance"
          "my Paris bag is stuffed with strawberries
          and the cool weight
          of glassed-in-fizz"

"the service was extraordinary"
                    "*a hand held discretely over my doubt;*
                        free wheeling around the clerestory"
"and good to catch up on the hovering angels—
for them our cares are marvellous"
                                "*something to play in the evening*
                                    just one small portion—

                            ★

I did not think,
        when I started on his blood
        of the efflorescence
        in its light

                    (a felt conundrum of the reddening, the white)

the host will feed you with three courses, with the sweetest at the start—

                                    and at the last—

all the telling in the world can barely write

                        —a single article, a syllable,
            drenched with elemental relevance.

                            ★

Here is the loop

her hands brought together
in a thunderclap of prayer

her eyes stitched together with pain
                through which you must dance

"her face in the half light was extraordinary"
                the sway of delectable waste

I wanted to love it   is part of the pleasure
and took you there early   of taking that chance

★

the ancient gods despaired of ever inventing invisible wings—

we've come back to this planet at great risk
    the burning latent in its juice—
the alternative channels, the slips and repeats
    cold flow
    of water on your tongue

    and the beautiful face you make when under the officer's
        thumb—

★

slowdown action of a dalliance
a withering
                    look, when she smiles at another
                the tightening cord. The crumbling walls
                she once thought liberating, made for,
                    howling gale and gusts of ash—

and cold ice flooding the body—

                the throat clamping credibly shut

I never wanted to go without!
                        —we're not going through with it now.

★

He's not of me, and yet

I recognise my features in the firmament

the roll of body acting against type

the natural fit becoming the unlovely—

here, your hair is ugly til it's covered

two deep slashes round the jaw

and when the swelling when the

when the swollen skin subsides—

you shall win beauty, have prizes

(sunlight filters in between the straw gaps of the roof)

★

The hours bend and slither to conclusion
          —it's three in the afternoon—
again—

too early, too late,
you never leapt the list
and slumber pooling in each unmoved limb—

with thoughts like marshflies landing on past projects
bloated, upturned, yet insistent on revisiting the surface—

when a lily livered frog
just might spring on you and kiss it.

★

Sit unsteadily in circles

  —the inner, the outer, a meshed collarette—

and breathe/ as an instrument /that's shivering in perpetuity;

  —thin silver sound becoming pure, like a feather dipped
    in ink

         —liquor, an opened vein

silence netting the remainder

and reminding you

"of the shot-through spaces:
prior to getting up—

          or the settling sky
      when you've turned the vision off—"

     ★

You're blue and able-bodied
with two antennae wending from the temples

picking up on sonic ruptures,
unintended misalignments
with a sixth or seventh sense

something other than telepathy,
sensitivity to friends

a tendency
to touch transgression

then shrink back, an overeager snail
who's encountered fluidity—

                              you remember
                    the tremors of my skin—

                    ★

when I was a child, I drew a silhouette
                    of a woman, arms raised, an S shaped curve
of her body like a shadow of the future
        —or a memory of what I was connected to,
formed in the oval of the womb—
                    and cradled in its kundalini energy—
around her form are psychedelic waves—
                    an emanating, taughtly-drawn fluorescence
        (bezel setting)
(the rainbowed remainder)

and I wrote instructions on it
for myself, as for another

you must go alone
get slimmer—

★

If you're not going
            to stumble down—

the hard hats
concrete balls
            will swing along—

do you remember, the small-girl-demolition—

            POW!ing into empty towers—

who heave—
      the thump of dissolution—
like a bullet in the gut—

                  or the letting out of doves—

Memento

This gift's in black and white,
bought on a whim in a foreign shrine,
Mary in all ages on the wrist:

he knew it would make you smile.
You stretch the simple bracelet
tight over your writing hand—

no question of force, her features
repeat, clack against wood beads
that interconnect her kitsch

gloss with loss of faith and its
(as if in glass reflection) half-
recovery; adore her iconography.

You get stunned by the glint of chains,
hints of sanctity in blades of grass
the terracotta army in the park

casting saints against nature;
he snaps you here and there
and in the final photograph

you open your arms. The light
streams down and blesses you:
everything else is pleasure.

Gemmology

gemstones with fractures and imperfections, though of less value in the jewellery trade, are regarded in alternative therapies as having self-healing properties which they can pass on to their wearer

Your heart

is a self-healing stone

the lines float feint

contain a razor blade

sharp to scar and halve

and half resolved

these gem pieces are much prized

(aspected cloud within the clarity)

a looser definition

of desirable; a crafted

artefact in lattice weave,

with a drafty rent punched through

where something

escaped, leaving

its sloshed wine stain.

Billow talk. A gush of black

where the bright squid isn't any more

putting you, decoy witness, off—

offering substance and pulse.

Untitled

It is too difficult to tell you
of my space, or of your need for it

To tally with the early revelations
chapter nine, verse two

Always we believe it is the end days;
infer a grand finale from the signs

What madness! Even thinking—
life will end! Ascension robes
like bridal are designed to be worn once.

Revelation can mean
almost anything. It is too easy

and it all depends
on whether you read
the last one word for word, or

like a magic eye, conjure between the lines
a kind of shining emptiness. It is

far too difficult to leave the thing alone.

Box Set

You're putting her life into boxes,
these days of the crunch
you need to be sure
of a holding position

the hollow strap of tape
binding each bash
wherein words lie
bundled into the dark

box after box;
base box sagging
with the piled-on response
a body, built under buckle—

some of this stuff,
is as if crumpled
in a poorwoman's safe,
vulnerable to plunder

magician's assistant; incipient mystic:
she is as if dismembered
prepped for hurried burial
and uncertain translation.

Dancing female tomb figure

The ritual defines her, lo,

she is my sad sung out my feather

light, my feather love. Your storm—

singing has been silent for so long;

grief glistens. The step

over the edge is dainty-free

and every hand a wish-bone,

every break a rendering that you

lie still under the earth to steady me.

Word Origin

Its etymology
is various—

French, some say,
a special sort of cup,

to hold a pledge
translucent to the sky;

or from a feather
pooling out its ink;

a siphoning
of essences together;

a hybrid
like a dark horse
in the field;

a mix of this—
a shaking of what was

into a new thing
fully of itself;

but I say only
as the morning breaks

that we have tasted it
and it is good.

Poetry etc: an unauthorised manifesto

Like a gull's egg, very light—a blink's splitsecond.
It's the dash that makes you human—

Here is the mouth closing—holding its portion of silence
in a pearly bite—a spark—a baby bird; the birth of myth. It
feathers being, the flame of the games.

By which ye shall know — for the sake of things unbidden.

You learn to perform tricks with the pen—holding it loosely,
wave between finger and thumb—that it seems to sway ((like a
wand)); a willow inclined by its nature to grieve.

And you as a child desired to be buried beneath it. Then you
learnt what that entailed—preferred a private baptism—

wet cross dousing, traversing the brow.

One breath's pressure on the surface of the world—a flutter
'gainst the glass.
A surge—as lucid as your dream—as though a bead of
meaning trickles down the pane—using each key—to form
harmonics, and sometimes, a melody.

O lean your brow against the condensation—and wait for the
word.

Your jacket's fitted, nipped in at the waist—your dress is
loose—so you wind a chain around the supple body—hang a
clarifying gem—

It attracts lucky dust — the skinny prints of memory.
Magnetise it if you must— I watch you slip it into fizz —

Take a sip on my account.

★

Look at the pattern of matter—the spiralling shell—

(the sound of the ocean's inside you, sussurring at will)

To hold these poems in your hand—is to sleep around a
soul—there's a sphere which defies explanation . . .

You're compelled to the leverage of language // anchoring
itself in ink.

Then again. You hear deletion pulsing at your throat—gentle
weather, enervation (we are turned like a handheld globe)
and the soul spills, shivers within—

Nothing changes but the quality of nothing. Like those early
evening hours—cut and fitted—and the poignancy of that.
When seconds sometimes seem elastic

. . . worth a single exhalation.

There's a tenderness in each machine—like the ghost you
thought you saw—like the cogs and wheels of fortune which
strike out the time you wasted—

There's a tenderness in water—but en mass, it's merciless—

You write while you're visiting its edge, the ions are negative,
the lesson—spraying its lace against your lips—

Gifts beneath the tree are slumped inside their boxes; are for
life. The kittens live inside your skin, and play with wool—

                              —and hook a loop of scribble on the page.

You need to let your reader use her fingers: skirl around you,
knit an intuition — second blink — and afterwards, a start—
to blue her eyes.

As a child, you drew a row of rings—like daffy bulbs in ether
white—each one the same, with the sketch of a rock on top.
Futurity was on your mind, because it's something you can
almost clasp—

(should another dimension allow you to fly—out of the two
which form the model of a box—)

                              ★

Wake up with a start!—who is she?

She left a well chewed toy. The sheets are crumpled by a
body, might be yours. You find tattoos upon your skin. You're
puzzled, at [not so much their message, as] the script they're
written in.

This one's for others, this, and this, and this—you step back,
contemplate your image in the glass.

The backward lends itself to contemplation:: moves from
the far out to the heart—a new polarity: the reverse pulse
of left-in text.

//a change is as good as a bed rest\\

while witty women writers got holed up—got plump on
milk—started to scrabble at the papertattered walls—

convinced a lady's trying to escape.

O cover your face—your black eyes are enough. You've learned
to look at strangers as a starting point—(for love?)— although
you dawdled on the day and now— it's late—

Some fellow struck the colours of the sunset. Nothing you put
on the table would reveal its point of origin.

"Now you mustn't kill the general—he sets the pace for work-
shy footmen. Only a hundred copies on this earth,"

The uncanny slips into itself, convinced that he's a living
being— if you word it strong enough ((the tide fans out and
feathers on treacherous sand))

"lest you grow weary—you grow weary—of his name."

The light railway = tracks of phosphorous = infinite
perspective in the dark.

Your vacant heart = = a bride, a simple verb == a ticket
stapled to a seat—

and the ruck of its language// intermittently banded.

As the platforms flash—I think her face superimposed

—in parallax//

★

Between believing a thing—and knowing a thing (that
chiaroscuro of old hope)—each phoneme turns to show a
profile. Holy pictures in a thumbnail.

How can you tell? They *look* like diamonds.

Roses underneath her feet.

You think the body's preservation is another act of faith—

The earth's core's origins are obscure, molten—only accessed
by a cipher: the twist of graphite into itself.

It's a question of paring down: for smaller and smaller, for lesser
for poorer; until the original zero postulates less than itself—

sits devoid, like a black pearl—like a black eye—

"I like to write between each assignation"
—the trudge of murder cases cakes your boots—

I start to wonder, do you think I'm looking old? It scratches
away, the patina of letters—ascribing something to the sheet—
and when you first hit gold, you bleed—

and when you break the pool of your skin, you weep—

a space drill—
the toughness of thin lines—
the axis of its charm kicks in—
the spinning weight between us—
like a glass lift, very bright—
and like the making of a name—
there is a danger in drawing—in drawing attention—

the aliens are out there.

These four walls allow the shields to fall to the dimensions of
the page.

★

Poetry as the sadness club? The anti-disestablishment of grief:

One small bird crashed into the glass—one limp line hanging in
the hand.
The jagged edge of childhood—you never forget your first
experiences; but like Byron,

you establish that much language

could twirl about the pulse.

To see you unhappy—is almost to intrude upon that mortal
knowledge—which is locked until the end—which the writer,

and the shrink, will whittle to a sliver.

A bundle of clothes hid in a box of tricks—the portrait and
the sitter, pretty—let's not give unwanted gifts—but only a
sense of pride—

"Books have the answer": so you weave your way, in a figure
of eight, to the second hand stacks.

A conversation with the dead and harried. Fingerprints of
itemised leavings, all sold out within the hour—

(nothing illegal, of course)

—but bars can allocate a space—a long draft of reflection . . .

The itch propels the pearl. The ones outside the shell are
malleable: keishi, lucid, sheer, and valuable.

—you'll have to wait through many curves of moon to have
enough, in truth, to wrap and unwrap skeins about the wrist,
and trail across a table cloth.

Leading you to me. Leading you over the edge—

A round for the captain! Eulogies for sport. "It was a grander
pastime ages gone," but now, laureateship's confined to
elegance: the royal signature—a crown with feathers in it

—and the power of the missed ship—
prisons rattling with the next in line.

Truth to tell the best investment
is the one made in your cells—

★

[the ones on the back row often do well]

It's difficult to tell when framed at the whiteboard: put them in
small groups and make the words work *hard*

—covert notes slipped into the arrangement—

the neophyte who makes the biggest splash;
an absent friend who's going to send it to you.

You'd think a casual approach—nevertheless, the setting up of
boundaries—

No, not late again, but misinformed: the cross connections,
broken links //
can leave you swinging like a Sunday bell.

I don't know how to read.

I didn't have the means to print it out, but saved it somewhere in
a drive—

Friendships come and go, but your date with the muse is always
a matter of trust. Or should that be tryst.

You walked around the whole of the room before your short
dance.
When once it is written, the steps get set down:

to the delicate tread of the heart—the delicate tread of the
heart—

the 'mark of the teacher'—like a wound, a sashay down the
corridor—
you leaf through yellow flags, and pink umbrellas, flattened by
their rain.

Voice is a creaking thing—it flaps and drags itself //over formica
//snuggles into leaden windows—

is itself, defying gravity and sun.

The monk said that in death
there is a shoal we never knew
flowing through the mesh of self—

a palimpsest of whispers—
like a flock of graduands—

you are sat as guardian, motley swathing your rough cut bones.
Palms clapping down.

★

A blessing on the psyche, and the soma, 'what you waited for'.
Nights of tapping—as though dowsing—for a stream of words—

Your hands stretch out across the table, touch the fingertips of
someone.
Make the sign of the poet. Cup the air: lift splayed fingers into
slanted rain

/ ... /

Habitual creatures, writers: like the steaming mug of coffee; like
the pool of light.
The Woolf at the door? A woman, at a table, writing.
Lap of voices, contrapuntal to a thought: a single whim becomes
the starting spell:

the letters, the letters, wanting to read them again—

   so a breath takes shape   so a sigh shapes flesh
     so an utterance betters the air   a loosely shifting coverlet
      a softbacked spine   translucent in the glow of it

      you take a sip   it makes you think of things
          and then forget.

         smiling just in case   it gets you nowhere

                 so a breath makes space.

A branch trembles imperceptibly; the soft snow falls.
A fence breathes, and its clutch of blue-white butterflies lift into
the sky—
these shifts are the action of the hand in dream, and the body of
its dreaming—

paler than you know—

I would like to write flowers into our promises.

★

Implicit all along . . . the skin of a writer gets etched.

But paper is always impossible, always available: drop small coins into the well, and get you gone.

The readers recline at their desks. Their bodies levitate into the night; their books spread wings. To espouse the encoding of height—

Presents fall onto the map—oft brush of the house's mouth. She has brought you the remnants of evening, as a plaything: you plan out your course—but know that the happiest meetings are often random.

Go over the range of concentric design. She had it all drawn out, you know.

It's rare to find—but when you do, the bonds unravel—and you've a sturdy theme within your grasp—

A holding cross: the wood smooth hewn and made for liminal hours.

You've had enough of verbal consciousness. And yet a broken quote is scrolled across, and another is complete.

So I ask you. Would you let him borrow another?

Knowing that you bear an equal weight of guilt—never returning what was leant.

Printed summons—on your license—like a badly sworn-in bishop—in a spurious basilica—there's no tasteful way to say it—

but the miracles—

★

Cut to the trill—you've played through the concerto, and the whole thing leads to grace.

Like the lessons said, there is inquiry on the part of silence —which you tiptoe around, and know you can sustain in friendship, being welcome and interpreted—each word a guest of the score—

a beautiful latecomer's catch / the simple frame sylphed sideways / so the light embroiders each entanglement.

Untitled

they stand a good chance
two brains, four lungs
two beating hearts
one blood supply

the longer the term
the greater chances of survival
(statistically better if they're girls)
you learn to adapt

though the cost implications—
the drain on time, resources
management issue: over
to you. stand together

you may feel slightly nauseous
but if you'd like to sign
here, and here, we'd be grateful.
not overdoing it, i hope.

we are tourists. could you
order a scan. i have family
over there. in here. everything else
like paperwork, was lost.

Pear Cut

she likes to cut things fine

to tread the shoulders of each line

as though a cat, padding

softly over potted wounds;

she likes to look at what she never

recognises as the loss of self,

enlarges each consumer window

chiefly to inspect the good she's bought.

the plump pear cut, set split on the wing,

is able, in its gallery, to splay

the tightest of white light

into fantastic simulated fire.

she's not concerned about the origin,

takes pleasure in delivery; in fact

would never order a soul about—

a typical woman.

Torque

the coolness of this silver
says it all

it sits in plenitude
and offers up

the bow of equal lips
each as though pierced

by tiny blue white hearts
immaculate

a teardrop
in a holy reliquary

a perfect shot,
the sliver of bright ice

(inoculating
for the open vein)

a slender space
across a finger's flesh

thus two hearts

separated
by the silence of a breath.

L'inconnue

*the unidentified young woman whose death mask became a popular fixture
on the walls of artists' homes after 1900*

you do not, could not know

that i died despairing of love.

the ice bright water might have been release

from a million jostling thoughts

unwelcome in a woman of my age;

the famous seine, a fatal surge

against philosophy's insanity.

you pulled me out, adored me

because i was complete in severance.

moulded, masked me, made

my face a mirror for your aching.

sixteen, artists guessed; too young

for any sort of line to score my heart;

i'm the holy maiden who said *no.*

here it is then; a prone girl,

folded into a poem, and then again.

you hold me down, as muse and now

your training model, thinly covered dummy,

a mock up with a mona lisa curl

to the lips. life saving boys
kiss and kiss again at the old myth.

now know i didn't die. i am
a girl who stepped in for another girl
who perished, inconsolable, who was
too damaged to be glorified in loss.
my pulse continues. oh that picture posed
early enough to let me take my gold.
the ice bright water. oh you do not know:

Schroedinger's Mystic

schroedinger's mystic: the nun in her cell

is hidden behind her flickering cloth &

answers/ doesn't answer questions set her.

torch the blessed curtain & she'll burn

or don't, & know she'll glow for love of god

who rests your soul in uncertainties & mysteries

while closing her eyes behind the white gauze

of her veil: so whether you are there or not

is of inconsequence, your prayer like lace

or sunlight filtering through & shifting place—

A Present

You placed the medal in my palm
to a slight shivering;
the proper response to a gift.

Cast to the time-honoured mould
her apparition asked
only that it's worn away

until, papyrus thin
like a dominated twin
atrophied in utero

it nuzzles into you, a nut
containing the potential
to glint your double self

throughout the lost spaces,
to here, delicate vow around the neck
a theory-shy butterfly wing

of what's surely not possible.

In Flux

I don't get it captain
this morning you told me
we mustn't tell the truth

but now I realise
that it's entirely possible
we are responsible

and running out of time
the sub-space fractures
are ripping us backwards

if it were me
(a questionable postulate)
I would have tried to warn you

"I cannot and will not
do anything to help you"
(give me your hand)

but now

declaring myself as hostage
We'll splinter the truth-lie layer
letting the light—

Untitled

In the woods, a blown whale slopes
to mourn each season: she's

impossible; a loner, massive,
iridescent bubble whose thin skin

could burst to the touch. An alien
who's swam so far that a flash

has pulsed her through to you
on your mulched-leave walk; how

ever to help? for what-in-heaven's there
could shiver any second;

settle; ram this big damp trunk
to utterly vanish. Noon. She moves,

a moon-cow; mouthless. Past
your range, while winter softens, sprays.

What It's Like

The sky in summer funnels down
that space between slate roof and redbrick walls
its blue expanse condenses
into whisps, a white essence
walking amongst us

like luck, or a revisiting of things
(kissing, the first time, on your urban balcony,
we two merged into the drag of traffic).
You never know what clouds
might remind you of:

a load of fables fit to bursting,
lizards set to flicker on a page,
the tongues of angels.
Absence, said to sharpen simile
is not what I welcome here.

You write in the dark, your hand on me
spells, in acute fluency:
an inverse Y, a wishbone,
rinsed with light at the margins of breath
and breath, and quite unbroken.

Citrine

Inside the band ring

you are experimenting

with the twist of claws

and the gradual of jewels

that sing in office: prime

sext, none, compline.

the gems refract daylight

making their own brand

of sunshine, magnifying

to a tear-burning ray.

Meditation

And if your mind is still enough
they rise to the surface, goldfish

attracted to a fingerdab, the flisk
of first intention. Whether you

risk the action of the wheel, there
will be whole rotation, corn

rippling in the fields, invisibility
as tangible as great waves of air.

Whether your mind is still enough
is barely the question, only that

body after body dances fast,
your skin absorbs all sorts of flare

into its fabric: there's romance,
pressed as delicate filigree

over the beating heart, and here
are the whispered words to say

(in local terms) how lovable;

the tongue to its brief phrases—

which settle on you like a butterfly

then flicker back, into infinity.

An Anchor

1

    (woman at a table holding her glass aloft to the light)
     —rough stone circles lucid through the ages—

dust and ashes of a child, and afterwards, another child

    —in which way are you just like me?—

She writes of a woman who nourished a vision
          how could this be?
  the *room without a window*:

a cluster of sunspot globes on high, the silver sheen

so far from what you could have seen.

2.

You like to sit here and imagine
how a woman back six hundred years

sees inside an aureole of flames
spies the future from a woollen veil

is astonished
loves to be—

but you delineate an understanding
which surpasses that of words,

the demarcations thought to be reality
and the structures of this world

in their subatomic flux
(you like to sit here

as she knelt and dreamt you)

Dear Reader

What is the probability
always assuming that life on other worlds—
swirling mist, singularity
of single signs; double suns

that it should evolve a body,
the bipedal vehicle,
gendered curve and angularity:
a round mouth below two bright eyes,

distinguished by the merely superficial:
colourings, the patterns of vocabulary
texted as alien henna, pierced
lip, hair plaited to infinity.

Let's splice the miraculous layer cake:
atmospherics. *Oxygen, earth, ocean*;
would same produce the shape of same?
or all those sci fi dramas—solipsism,

a concave mirror vicing the globe
of poor souls perusing themselves.
I'm looking at you. So fortunate we
found each other: *I, you: you and I.*

Sabbatical

The problem with travelling on Sundays
                              (lope of transit past the mist of grass)
is the slant of light—
            which
                        unlike the weary, the family passengers,
                              the poets hogging the tables, each one single
(with their ruched black bags and coffee)—

the glancing slant of light
that finds you out—
                        while you huddle in the corner of the carriage

sleepy sunlight like a fractious child
playing with tart/sweet butterfingers

                                          across a shiny screen
                              the furrow of your brow—

                        ★

ceremony slips here—
(the oily thought of it, the herb-scattered heretic floor)

she sits enthroned, but you— you are a traveller,
your short skirt flutters in the prayers

your ears are hooped with praise
while the congregation greys itself to nothing

and the trinkets in your hand ready to raise:
  "the empty church is so much more appealing than the full"

you start to unpeel the flesh of it
it spins to words that rhyme abominably
then comes undone
to rest in quiet

★

I didn't hear any firing, but
                    the coloured lights unclench in pitch black
withal the pilgrims stuttering

        //performative maths, the Ave abacus//
sustaining this universe's chantry
                "this is the bed in which I dreamt of you"

and here the dining table where I wanted stronger wine
men in a circle, their faces like petals.
                        He doesn't. He does.

An Encounter

He breaks into the carriage
at five past noon;

and you are just thinking
how dirty the windows

look as the train creaks
on through sunshine—

Don't you know (he's loud)
where this one goes?

an old couple
turn their heads, murmur,

and you ask yourself
if you should be afraid.

He doesn't like your shades:
he tells you, *take them off,*

so you fold their mirror screens
into your lap.

Tell me he says, *the words*
of the Lord's Prayer

and you don't miss a beat
but go: *Our Father . . .*

the man crumples opposite
and fits his voice to yours

until it finishes. *Amen.* And then
he lunges towards you:

raise your hands but
you can't stop his lips

connecting with your face.
God bless you he says; his

breath is raw. There's
light and banded shadow

and then he is gone.

Holy Pictures

he undresses her in front of the mirror
she follows the flow of his hands,
in the half light, everything is flickering
as though there is a candle in her body
and its flame's starting to show.

the layers drop away, the glow of them
is a new identity, the merge
of heat and skin defined by that
reflected double; naked couple
like a child who, seeing its reflection

is amazed at who it might be, who
it is. he lifts her hair and feathers it;
her figure is a deep blue inner fire,
the blonde an aureole around,
the glass their fluid iconography.

here's the stage they step towards:
man, woman, vulnerable, waving,
like a plaque sent into space—
but then they turn, as does the wardrobe door,
each free to fall all over again.

Underground

it was worth the slip
to be caught in arms
as that low slung escalator
juddered us down.

language on the platform
wandered where it would;

against the general crowd
your rough blue coat,
the silver ball-and-hoop
in the crease of your ear.

Mediumship

A moment of quiet, please,
gentlemen, ladies,

while I try to draw the two worlds

                closertogether—

who can tell me

here's a shimmer, like the taste of icing sugar,
silk-dust skin of a long-gone swimmer

the gentleman I have who's coming through

talking about a field full of flags

each marking a significant encounter.

you, madam, would you try to understand,
why he's holding a mirror, face towards you—

not a sign of vanity I'm sure,

nor indeed Medusa at the fair (you'll flutter a laugh, forgive me)

And what's the story with the word 'permission'
which he wants me to repeat he offers you?

it's easy to feel queasy on the platform,
do remember to breathe. What if I said the word

recalcitrant? illumination? blow?

the spirit where it listeth. Sweet, don't cry.

a fading spray is barely a surrender,
and I leave its love with you.

Phase Transitions

It's the softness of the shifts which take her;
        a branch trembles imperceptibly
                and the piled snow falls

Light clarifies into ice,
        sweet pink, at the point of dissolution
                becomes sudden water

A sun drenched fence is as if breathing;
        a clutch of blue-white butterflies
                lift into the sky

A lucky clover spins,
        splayed out in the air
                the wind takes it

one carnation blooms
        the blush of its petals
                are tinged with gold

And she is as if flying
        Rescued from the gruel of the mountain
        Where, in the far distance,
                The whole earth turns.

Lecture Notes

Enter when ready.

                              —((whoosh—
the door undone: an armistice with your reality,
tread of lost seeds into threadbare texture,

cast a cold remedy, a diffuse panacea
it numbs the most distressing of the symptoms,
exacerbating others

                              —check it out:
                              an unfamiliar name

                    ★

such a gorgeous glossy rulebook!— nestled in the centre of
the waxworks—
                    the spark of the game's in its stillness

you could have your photo taken,
your soul would hardly notice
how many admirers whisper

                         —in the corner of the camera—

                         a ghost face, seeped into the
                         body,

                         as a blind mannequin
                         punches the pane.

                    ★

her mouth's a splendid artifice = two ways to read it

                        —rictus affirmation—

the pulse of a bird on the wing of your breath
she tips it against the ivory inch
the "agony of irony" in fiction

tripping over the wall, skirts multiplying
as a blushing angel holds his wings

"Is that an arrow?"

feather your quiver of fingers at the clouds.

                    ★

it pays to be // to orchestrate becoming
ambition's splay is what it's all about // the list of gold to the font
the lip of god overarching the fountain //crystal limits
                        cutting lapidary terms
                        she whispers implications
                  in the smallest natural print
                  an ant to the slaughter
                    march of the marginal tab

                    your check's unbalanced
            // past the post

                ★

the peach of your flesh is
extraordinary—look how life flushes under the sun

a tie can indicate your personality

the knot's a satin rush; a pool of silk to the lap
the way the hand alights like grace about the throat

I wish the pendant matched most / <u>everything</u> she wears
then the differences

                       the would-be jewelful—

          ★

after a death the prose slows up.
the mortuary keeps its sake
the drawers pulsed shut.
each sheet's a swish redundancy
(and I thought I had signed what you ask me to sign)
there's something trying to land
I twist my vanquished hand in semaphore
and can't believe there's more to mark
the swirl when you close my lids—
divine

          ★

look at the sliver of doubt for the liver//
                             one too many shifts of vision—

not to trust the eyes, when fiery particles
blister on the inside of your veins.

you watch
—*you ticking clock*—
           reach a new sphere with the pressure puffer

                        the head of a kitten on his shoulders!

(always the other civilization
 has the dogs' heads)

                             ★

on the record or not at all— the fabric of imaginative recall's
unrivalled
                             (her unravelled hair)

 a slow, even tempered delivery.

 an early morning raid—

"the taste of egg stays me— the knowledge I got from
domestic circumference"

—touch of the river though, in a head like that—

★

        the address you wanted's on your desk
      beside the pile of slow-subsiding footnotes
     beside the drained cup and denuded sprig
      behind the heaviest of tomes and the
  statements delayed their moment of deliverance

I sit behind and to the left of you
texting insights intermittently

I love localities:
you are beside yourself.

            ★

just look at the wickedly fit
by the time you get it

get to the end of your term

small knees
          pulsing at the chora
          you are liable to all sorts of infiltrating
thoughts—   the souls around a hospital
          spick and span, except for the loose sluts' wool:
          "you're playing cat's cradle with the primordial"

          —another notch on the dial—

★

I am slipped, I am sudden
am a ring around the neck of it

I'm telling you a story, in order to keep my mind

and did you know between the concentric
lies the inscrutable angelic

a hagiographic splash between the bindweed of the years
and the ghost of a chance that this means

                                        (an ellipsis of an answer)

★

"it's not that I'm against the idea, just don't want to join a club"

                        even societies that predicate upon a paradox

    the loss of family, the pulse of cell into cell
                                        (community of solitaries)

an undertaking to embrace a certain form
                        —appropriate the asymmetric rule—

the queasy flecks of photocopied hope

                            (look thirsty: have another think)

★

dig the little links of each new cuff
and turn away your cheek

slice of insight—

                  modern loop around a chastened block

                     —those bowls of midnight food—

women wan like ghosts

and like the spirit trapped in a dead husk

the discomfort of witness

         —the shudder of uttering, shackled premise—

"I wanted to tell you—the mystery of faith—"

a gesture of slender wrist, its shimmer.

★

"all I can say is when I'm having mine, the lights go dimmer"
                    = so the dancing isn't awkward?

the shape of things is lucid as a silhouette that passes over water

a table for women and their daughters and
the men with gifts to hand
the drape of lyric like a shawl
for those whose move it isn't—

★

do you want to be matched by your shadow?

//the challenge of each filament, bonded to its opposite//
caused and causing like the snake-&-tail
{a loveknot's venom and its antidote}
then programme the text to respond like wildfire—

smouldering charcoal in its wake
— as you lie there, puppeteer of mine—

★

it's awkward being among the first,
arriving too early, we dither
reconsider slipping outside for a drink
—but there's never enough of an hour to go—

and all the inside wine's for charity
good sir, we must have met twenty-one years ago or more

// I'm shot back to the leaving do at school//
"each stage the turn of the lost:

this time it's the last"

★

your face, imprinted on the monitor
subliminal, gorgeous, heterodox, by god
you're mouthing a word, his name
the picture's crackling, rent by greyscale
                              ((gone))
and I, the convalescent scholar-in-his-bed
                    press stop, press play again, press stop—
your profile's flaxen intermission

—I look up into his eyes, and type—

★

"so how do you like it madame?"
                    —the feather cut—
the bringing in of layers
                    —your body enhancing procedures—

smelling like citrus, like butter, like light—
                    it floods to the side of the booth
                    my sight obscured by your snip

★

//a few lines, from her recipe—
I listen out for word of birds//

*

"I love that programme, the actors work so wonderfully
together, don't they?
the dark rooms, the clanging doors
                              the dim-lit secret observation post

it's just that the plots get *so* convoluted
I watched it with my husband and *he* couldn't follow it all
but of course you can enjoy it on other levels

the pace of it; the killer banter—"

*

there was a student with a snake: it rested amicably on her head—
until after the class when she would dance to the pulse of something
louder than verse

the circle and the vertical—// inspired him//—

*

If you have the time
                   you could create the look!

//—the palimpsest of glances which congratulate a page— //

the slipper which could act as sign of faith,
wax in the chapel, warmly lyrical
the glow of a well trodden path:

all this promotes belief in substance

as each atom blinks and glimmers
spookily

★

one long weekend spools a life
one day plunges a heart to debt
oh tell me, was it worth the wait

exact suspension of a song
committed to the processed body
saved online, a consecration (you can always press!)

the hallucinogenic quality of twilight
after twilight: the man wasn't ready, but
acting wishfully before completion's—

★

able bodied elephants   bending the knee

I wrote my questions leaning on your exercise book

                              and shuddered wine over my back
                              the spray was cooling, not unpleasant

your appetite for vegetables withered straight away

who'd walk into a door
when waiting outside's so nice?

                              ★

the study of hullabaloo
                              —*an intermediate module*
twins itself with infinite jiggery pokery

your eyes doing the rounds
                              —your c.v. shredded,

you wait for a rise, you plummet into grace,

you practise smiles and other gestures designated for this place—

                    and they take you on the off chance.

                              ★

"I can't contact those beyond the bedclothes"
the scoop of her neck elongating its line

her textual desire—is intermittent—like a sparking fire—
the curl of the burn—the spit of the hot spot—

interlinking London like a cybernetic pentacle

 coffee singes the synapses—the torch of an accompanying
tune—

★

the trilogy is the lest selfish of settings—
mother, father, baby doll—
the slope of cornucopia—

                                        and the pouring rain—

                        there in the bell curve is his splinter—
                                    an urgent extraction—
                        dab with the better of two halves—

but once you start on that collision course—
the bad hand waving you through—

                no point in moping on your own

★

(a splendid attitude)

plastered, with a louche intention
ah ha! the marbling of living paper

/one year on's an anniversary /
you fold up in unusual ways—

but unless you're hammered tissue thin
only so many misprisions

every print looks like an animal's—
a parliament of doves or crows

                              ★

and his messages weren't getting through
        —the transit necessarily a path that's kind of walked alone—

he's called but she's been busy getting back to surface ground
        —and it seemed, even then, to still be summer—

the framed paintings waiting there
        — a particular deep of blue—

        and quietly)), the intimate distance between